By using this journal, you understand that it is not meant to diagnose, treat, prevent, or cure any disease. It is not a substitute for care from a licensed physician or therapist. Do not stop medication or treatment with your provider without speaking to your provider first. You further understand the content of this book and sessions are not medical, financial or romantic advice, and should not be used as a substitute for medical or professional advice. Please discuss life-changing choices with certified or licensed professionals.

This journal is for informational purposes only and is not intended to be medical advice, diagnosis, treat, prevent or cure any disease. The information in this journal is not an alternative or substitute to medical advice from your doctor or other licensed healthcare providers. If you have specific questions about any medical matter, including nutrition, supplements, or lifestyle changes, you should consult your doctor or other licensed healthcare providers.

Copyright © 2020 Stacee Magee

All rights reserved. No part of this book may be reproduced or used in any manner without the prior written permission of the copyright owner,
except for the use of brief quotations in a book review.

To request permissions, contact the publisher at
support@spiritfluent.com.

First paperback edition December 2021.

Art by Stacee Magee and the amazing people at Canva

Printed by Spirit Fluent Books in the USA.

Spiritfluent.com

Please Remember:

This journal is designed to support your journey but not replace the care of a licensed practitioner or therapist. In this journal, I deal in the spirit. Please consult your doctor for matters of the physical. Nothing in this journal, our social media accounts, group calls, or other affiliations is meant to diagnose, treat, prevent, or cure any disease. It is not a substitute or replacement for care from a licensed physician or therapist.

This journal is dedicated first to my soulmate who supported my healing journey and second to all of my amazing clients who have loved and supported me and made Spirit Fluent into the stuff that dreams are made of.
I love you!

Before You Begin a Message About Mental Health

You are a Spiritual Human on a learning journey in a world not designed for spiritual success and healing. We are often told to ignore our intuition or spiritual messages.

If it can't be seen, touched, or quantified by science, it must not be real. We are often told that spiritual awakenings are a mental health crisis. Sometimes, a mental health crisis can mimic a spiritual awakening or come alongside it. The best way to tell the difference is by asking yourself these simple questions.

1. Are the spiritual messages or experiences pushing you towards doing something good? Like healing, helping yourself or others, etc.? Do I feel like I am heading down a path of light, expansion, and growth?
2. Is my spiritual experience pushing me into self-harming behaviors, hurting others, or doing dangerous/harmful things? Is my awakening causing more harm than good?

Suppose you resonated with question one more - you are doing good. Keep going!

If you resonated with number two more, it might be time to seek the support of a counselor or therapist on your journey. There is nothing wrong with getting help as you walk your spiritual path, and no, medications won't impede your progress. So don't be afraid to seek support on your journey.

This Spiritual Shit Show Belongs to...

There is no rhyme or reason to this shit show of a journal. So open the pages and trust that the Universe will guide you to the shit you need to know. There may be some minor fuck-ups along the way, a misspelled word or two, ignore them because life is imperfect, this journal is imperfect, and so are you.
And that's ok.

With Love,
Stacee

You're here for a reason, and I'm going to tell you some stuff about you.

You're probably a giving person, but you get burned because sometimes you provide too much, or you burn out.

You probably have childhood trauma or deep generational trauma that needs healing, but you've been ignoring it.

Random people come up to you all the time and ask you for advice, and you have no idea why. The reason is that you have spiritual gifts but never thought it was actual or possible.

You have been trying to figure out who you are or what your purpose is for a long time. You are almost at your point of giving up, but somehow, you get up and try each morning.

You may have ADHD, Autism, or other neurodivergent tendencies.

You know that you are meant for something much more than what you are doing right now, but you are unsure of how to get there.

You probably have a chronic illness you have been trying to heal for a long time.

If this is you, my spiritual human, I want you to know that you are in the right place. Spirit Fluent is a gathering place for spiritual humans, and I am your guide, Stacee Magee. Join me as I guide you on your spiritual journey of healing the body, mind, and soul.

Most of us have felt misunderstood and confused about that question our entire lives. We have wanted to discover something greater within ourselves. To communicate in the language of your soul, you need to go within to see the divinity within you.

The spiritual gifts you were born with are a part of your soul and intended to assist you on your journey, helping fulfill your soul's purpose, mission and learning what you need to from your human experience. There will be different gifts for each of us. Some will have many, some will have few, some will share the same gifts with you, and some will have different gifts.

You are born with some abilities and others you develop, but I genuinely believe that all gifts are available to those who seek them.

Centering and Grounding Your Energy.

Before you start this journal, ground your energy and create your shield. This will help you create stronger protection as you continue your healing process.

1. Take a seat in a comfortable chair or on the ground. Make sure your feet are flat on the floor. Place both hands on your lap.

2. Listen to your heartbeat while you close your eyes.

3. The three-breath technique is done by inhaling through your nose and exhaling through your mouth while placing your tongue slightly behind your front teeth on the roof of your mouth. Become aware of your breath in relation to your heartbeat. You should take a breath in for a count of three, then exhale for a count of three. Repeat this three times.

4. Slowly take a deep breath in and out. Notice that your heart rate follows your breath and feel your thoughts relaxing now. Continue to slow down your breathing until you feel calm, relaxed and develop a warm, pleasant sensation in your belly. Only when you achieve this will you realize what it means to be "centered."
Once centered, move on to creating your shield.

Shielding

Shielding your energy is like wearing shoes when you go outside for protection. It protects you against energy vampires and other energies that can be overwhelming spiritually. Check out my YouTube channel Spirit Fluent for a great video on energetic shielding.

When setting your protection, remember these four steps.

1. What does your shield look like? What color and shape is it?
2. What is your shield doing? What is it protecting you from?
3. How strong are your shields? Is anyone allowed beyond it?
4. . How long is your shield to stay in place? Where is your shield drawing its energy from?

Spiritual Self Defense and Protection

How does my personal protection shield look and feel?

What are my home protection shields like?

What else can I do to protect myself, my home, family and workspace?

Spiritual Self Defense and Protection

Draw a picture of your personal shield to remind yourself of the type of protection you are creating.

Journal Shit Here

You Will Experience Three Things as You Heal on Your Spiritual Journey:

1. As you heal, people will come on your journey and support you. These are the ones that will lift you and keep you going.
2. Some people will fade out of your life; they won't align with your journey. You may lose people from your life which will feel challenging, but release them with gratitude.
3. And then there are the narcissistic assholes who will try to keep control over you. They will do anything they can to stop your healing and stop your spiritual journey.

Those people are the ones whom you'll want to burn the motherfucking bridge down. Free yourself from them and your life, and keep walking forward on your healing path.

People I Need to Release From My Life...

Which people in your life are vampires, and why should you remove them from your life?

Burn this Page

Shit I'm Grateful For

SHIT THAT MAKES ME HAPPY

1. ....
2. ....
3. ....

SHIT THAT MAKES ME GRATEFUL

1. ....
2. ....
3. ....

EVEN THOUGH LIFE FEELS LIKE A SHIT SHOW, WHAT IS GOOD ABOUT TODAY

Journal Shit Here

Journal Prompts

What are ways you can listen to Spirit?

Can I give myself permission to listen and trust?

How can you make your spiritual messages more clear?

How can you follow the guidance of Spirit today?

Spirit Journaling

Try this before or after meditation. Set your intentions to connect to your higher power or higher self. Still your mind and write a letter, like writing home to a loving parent ask for guidance on whatever you need. Then flip this page over, become still once more, and write whatever comes to your heart or mind. You may find your questions have been answered!

Journal Shit Here

Shit I'm Grateful For

SHIT THAT MAKES ME HAPPY

1. ....
2. ....
3. ....

SHIT THAT MAKES ME GRATEFUL

1. ....
2. ....
3. ....

EVEN THOUGH LIFE FEELS LIKE A SHIT SHOW, WHAT IS GOOD ABOUT TODAY

Types of Clairs
A QUICK REFERENCE GUIDE FOR SPIRITUAL SHIT

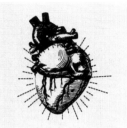
Clairempathy
(Clear Emotions)

Clairtangency
(Clear Touching)

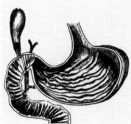
Clairsentience
(Clear Feeling)

Clairvoyance
(Clear Seeing)

Claircognizance
(Clear Knowing)

Clairgustance
(Clear Tasting)

Clairsalience
(Clear Smelling)

Clairaudience
(Clear Hearing)

Clairintellect
(Clear Understanding)

Other Types of Spiritual Gifts

- Wisdom Keeper
- Healer
- Warrior of Light
- Truth Seeker
- Feeling/Touch
- Music/Song
- Kindness/Friendship
- Connections to Animals or Nature
- Knowing/Understanding
- Discernment/Truth knowing
- Feeling/Body
- Language
- Prophecy/ Knowing the Future
- Dreams and Interpretation of Dreams
- Visions
- Spiritual Healing
- Smelling
- Whispers of the Spirit
- Weather/Environment
- Organization/Structure
- Knowledge/Wisdom
- Guidance/Teaching
- Discovery/Creation
- Art/Creative
- Writing/Communication
- Singing/Music
- Spiritual Hearing/Sound

Journal Prompts

What is the language of your soul?

What spiritual gifts do you recognize in yourself?

What spiritual gifts do you wish you had?

What spiritual gifts do you not want to have?

Listen to Your Heart

When we practice heart coherence, we exist in the "now" and not in the future or the past. This is because heart coherence implies unconditional acceptance of what is. This has the effect of making us feel whole without requiring an escape from anything.

With heart breath, you will experience healing and balance from the heart. With your physical, mental, and emotional systems aligned, you'll be able to access the intuitive guidance from your heart.

Learning to activate and control the breath of your heart creates a profound shift in you that lets you handle situations with more emotional balance, compassion, and clarity.

This awakens you to your higher self, releases old emotions and trauma from your heart, and opens communication to the divinity within.

Journal Prompts

Write about emotions using the following prompts:

What are my emotions telling me?

Is this something that is real or my fears speaking?

What do I need to let go of?

The Care and Feeding of Spiritual Humans

Becoming a spiritually gifted human isn't easy, learn what you need to stay healthy and well.

If you're in the midst of a spiritual awakening, learning what you need to eat, drink and do to stay healthy and well can be challenging.
If you've been feeling like something is different about you lately, it's probably because there is.

Becoming a spiritually gifted human isn't easy. It takes work to stay healthy and well in our bodies, minds, and spirits. Here are some things you can do to take care of yourself during a spiritual awakening:

1) Get enough sleep—You may not need as much sleep as you think, but everyone needs at least 7-8 hours of quality rest every night. The body heals itself and the mind clears during sleep so it's important to get enough sleep so that your body can do what it needs to do while you're resting.

2) Practice self-care—Self-care is essential for any kind of healing process so make sure that you're taking time out of each day (even if it's just 15 minutes) to take care of yourself in some way: maybe it's meditation or maybe it's a bath with candles; whatever works for you! Just remember that taking care of yourself will allow your body and mind to heal more quickly than if they were left alone in their own devices all day long!

3) Be mindful—Being mindful means being aware of what's happening around us at all times without judgment or attachment.

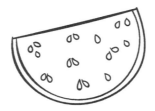

I know it can be really hard to take care of yourself when you're going through a spiritual awakening. It used to be that villages and tribes would take care of their healers, shamans, and medicine people—but now we're thrown to the wolves.

It's not that no one cares about us anymore; it's just that society doesn't know how to handle us. And that's okay! But if you're feeling like you need some TLC right now, here are some things you can do to take care of yourself during your awakening:

- Eat meatless meals more often. Many people find that eating meat becomes harder after awakening, I know I did! If you find that foods your used to eat before your awakening just don't sit well anymore, listen to your body. I know I craved things like watermelon and lots of sweet potatoes, which are both high in magnesium and potassium (magnesium and electrolytes are often the things that are depleted in the spiritually gifted because of all the spiritual energy going through use). Remember: You are a conduit of light!

Cantaloupe is a superfood

It contains a range of antioxidants, including selenium, beta carotene, vitamin C, lutein, zeaxanthin, and choline. Growing up in the Desert Southwest one of my favorite treats is Agua De Melon which many of the incredible local cooks make to go along with the spicey Latino food they serve. I honor them for teaching me a fun way to experience one of my favorite foods.

I have made this a part of my morning routine with a fun twist by freezing the canteloupe and making it into a smoothie! It really does start my day off with an energy boost! Try this when you need an energy boost or to start your day.

Agua de Melon Smoothie

Ingredients:

-2 cups of frozen cantaloupe (You can also use fresh), skinned, seeded, and cut into chunks

-2 cups of water

-Juice 1 lime (or lemon)

-Stevia or Agave to taste (optional)

Directions:

Combine all ingredients in a blender and blend until smooth. Pour into a large pitcher and enjoy!

Electrolyte Watermelon Drink

I often see spiritual people who are dehydrated or have electrolyte imbalance because of all that spiritual energy coursing through our bodies. This recipe will help you get back on track with some potassium, magnesium, and other trace minerals.

Watermelon is 92% water, making it the perfect fruit to help stay hydrated. It's also full of vitamin C and antioxidants, which can help boost your immune system.

But sometimes we need a little help getting the nutrients we need—and that's where this recipe comes in!

Here's what you'll need:

6 cups cubed (2lb) chilled Watermelon

1/8 tsp Real Salt or Celtic Sea Salt

Try adding some mint or lime for a variation

Have you ever wondered why people seem so much happier when they're around plants?

The answer is all in the enzymes! Ok its more than that, but stay with me here!

Enzymes are the bridge between the physical and the spiritual world. They help us digest our food and metabolize it into energy, but they also play a role in every single function of your body. Enzymes are what make life possible.

In fact, before the introduction of GMOs, food irradiation, microwaving, and food processing, humans used to get more enzymes from their diet—and as a result, we're able to better absorb nutrients from their food. But now that we've been introduced to these new methods of cooking and preservation, we're losing our enzyme supply at an alarming rate. And that's not good for anyone! It can lead to malnutrition and other health issues down the line if you aren't careful about stocking up on them now (see below).

So how do you get more enzymes? The best way is by eating raw foods like fruits and vegetables and supplementing with a probiotic like Digestive Enzymes, I have some resources listed on my website to give you some ideas.

Enzymes are a powerful tool that can help you stay healthy and avoid illness. Most people have heard of them, but don't know exactly what they do or how they affect the body. If you want to keep your body functioning at its best, here's what you need to know:

Enzymes break down diseased parts of the body, allowing the body to return to its normal condition. This means that if you have an injury or illness, it's especially important to use enzymes to help heal your body more quickly and efficiently.

Enzymes have blood purifying action that eliminates metabolites in the bloodstream, which can cause many different problems including pain and inflammation. If you find yourself feeling those two things regularly, talk with your medical provider about adding enzymes into your diet—they may just be what you need!

Enzymes have cellular rejuvenating action that promotes the regeneration of damaged cells. This means that if your cells aren't working as well as they could be (which happens naturally over time), enzymes may be able to help get them back on track!

If this resonates with your, alk with your medical provider about adding enzymes into your diet—they may just be what you need!

Becoming a spiritual human isn't easy, and you might find yourself feeling a little lost.

I've been there!

Here are some things you can do to take care of yourself during a spiritual awakening:

1. Find your community. You don't have to go it alone! Find other people who are going through similar experiences, and learn from each other. Hint: Spirit Fluent has an amazing community we are growing, visit SpiritFluent.com/community for more info!

2. Make sure you're getting enough sleep and eating well. If you're not taking care of your physical body, then it's harder for your spirit to be strong and healthy too.

3. Don't worry too much about what others think of your gifts or abilities—you'll learn more about them as time goes on anyway! Just focus on honing in on what feels right for YOU in the moment, and let everything else fall away into the background noise of life that it really is.

-Listen to your body. If certain foods don't sit well with you anymore, if you find yourself craving something like watermelon or sweet potatoes (which are both high in magnesium and potassium), then listen up! Your body is telling you something important about what it needs.

-Take breaks from social media and technology. We live in a world where we are constantly connected through our phones, computers, TVs... even lights! It can be draining on the soul because all these things take away from time spent in nature or even just being alone with ourselves. So when possible, turn off those electronics!

Carrot Juice

Every morning before I went to school, my grandparents and parents insisted that I drink a glass of carrot juice. Only now do I know exactly how restoring and healthy it is for the body. Some have said that it is high in vitamins B, C, D, E, G & K, and my grandmother always claimed it would help us resist infection and cleanse out our bodies. In addition, she claimed it would give us a long life and prevent us from getting all sorts of diseases. It is still one of my favorite juices, and sometimes I'll throw some beet or apple in with it when I juice in my vintage Champion Juicer. There's nothing better than a glass of carrot juice in my opinion.

What is your favorite juice for healing?

Journal on What You Can Change in Your Life to Nourish and Strengthen Your Body...

The Care and Feeding of Spiritual People

Taking good care of your body as you awaken is important, so try these ways to support your journey.

Raw fruits and vegetables & nourishing foods with high vibration are perfect for spiritual humans like you. Since ancient times, adaptogens have been used by spiritual people to deal with stress and increase energy. Ashwagandha and Rhodiola Rosea are two of my favorites, but I also like Tulsi (Holy Basil), Ginseng, Schisandra, Turmeric, Goji Berry, Cordyceps, Licorice, and Reishi.

Trace minerals, Electrolytes, and Magnesium are often depleted in spiritual humans, so supplement where appropriate. Remember it's ok to be an unhealed healer if you are working on healing yourself. However, if you ignore your healing, it can spell disaster. Get your physical ailments diagnosed and treated by a functional medicine doctor or naturopathic doctor to help support your healing.

A qualified therapist can help when you experience trauma, grief, or mental/emotional pain that won't go away. As "holistic psychology" is becoming more popular, you may even find one trained in functional psychology.

As a spiritual human, it's easy to burn out and cause dysfunction at night, making you feel tired all the time, and tired spiritual people have a hard time helping themselves or others. Before you go to sleep, try meditating or listening to relaxing classical music. You can get better sleep with Melatonin, Ashwagandha, L-Theanine, Magnesium, and other natural shit. Just check with your doctor to make sure it's safe for you.

The Care and Feeding of Me

Journal about how you can take care of and nourish your body today

Journal Shit Here

Body Scan

Some days you will feel like absolute shit. You may want to spend the entire day in bed with a bag of potato chips watching Hallmark movies. That is OK for a day, maybe two, but it's time to become self-aware if it goes beyond that. Understand what your soul is trying to tell you.

Close your eyes. Take a deep breath in through your nose and out through your mouth. Starting with the top of your head, become aware of how your body feels. Slowly move down your body, noticing how each body part feels, down to your toes. Observe any physical or spiritual discomfort in the areas below that you see or feel. Draw a face that represents how you feel right now.

Self Care

A Spiritual Awakening will make you feel fucked up and imbalanced. By incorporating some of these activities (or similar) into your life, you can take some of the edge off of this crazy spiritual journey you are on. To create balance, you need physical and spiritual self-care.

Pick one item from the list and incorporate it into your daily routine, adding another when it comes naturally. It will be overwhelming if you try to do too much at once. If you miss a day, try again tomorrow.

Spiritual

Prayer
Meditation
Journaling
Grounding
Tai Chi
Volunteer
Forgiveness
Religion
Reiki
Energy Healing

Physical

Exercise
Spa Days
Hiking
Nourishing Foods
Vitamins
Massages
Acupuncture
Yoga
Vacation
Organize/Clean

Drink Your F-ing Water

Depending on whom you ask, your body is made up of 70-90% water. Water not only helps your body stay physically hydrated but spiritually as well! Water allows our energy to flow through our body the way we need to be healthy, happy and balanced in life.

Did you know that drinking a glass of water first thing in the morning is said to be able to wake you up just like a cup of coffee?

After you wake up each morning:
1. Stretch and get out of bed.
2. Do your morning prayer/meditation ritual.
3. Drink a full glass of water.

Most importantly, take a minute to pause and think about how amazing the water makes you feel. Then, remember to stay hydrated during the day by keeping water with you wherever you go!

Journal Prompts

Healing the Wounded Healer

What are you ready to heal today?

Name ten ways you can start taking better care of yourself.

How would you show up as your totally healed self?

Journal Shit Here

Shit I'm Grateful For

SHIT THAT MAKES ME HAPPY

1. ....
2. ....
3. ....

SHIT THAT MAKES ME GRATEFUL

1. ....
2. ....
3. ....

EVEN THOUGH LIFE FEELS LIKE A SHIT SHOW, WHAT IS GOOD ABOUT TODAY

Tattoos Are Healing

That tattoo on your butt is not there for the reason you think. I'm going to tell you why your tattoos have the power to heal trauma from emotional, generational, and physical pain. Tattoos actually hold more power and meaning than even the people who got them understand. When you get a tattoo, it shows that you have a deep need to heal from something or someone or an experience, and sometimes they are ancestral. Still, in all ways, they are healing. Where you get your tattoo will tell you and me what you were healing from when you got that tattoo. It may not actually be the reason that you thought you wanted to get that tattoo. So that matching tattoo with your best friend on your butt doesn't actually mean best friends forever. It means that you were healing trust issues.

Journal about what your tattoo means to you here.

Mindless coloring, fill these lines with colors. Use the first colors you grab, no peeking. Colors have meaning. Notice what colors you chose and what they mean.

Colors

1. Red is the frequency of our Basic/Root chakra, which is located at the base of our spine. Red heals pain and increases mental clarity.
2. The Sacral chakra vibrates at the Orange frequency. Orange is happiness and kindness.
3. The Solar plexus chakra vibrates with the frequency of Yellow. Yellow is the color of inspiration, good ideas, warmth, and cleansing.
4. The Heart chakra vibrates with the frequency of green. Green acts as a powerful cleanser and can be used to heal illnesses.
5. The Throat Chakra vibrates with the frequency of Blue. The color blue dissolves sickness and is the color of empathy.
6. The third eye chakra vibrates with the frequency of Indigo. Intuition and understanding are associated with this color.
7. Violet is the vibration frequency at the top of the head, the Crown chakra. It is our connection with the spiritual world and our higher power.
8. White is the master healer, the color that embodies all colors.
9. Gold is the color of joy, wisdom, and knowledge. It is the amplifier of colors like a disco ball reflecting light.

What do these colors mean to you?

Your Spiritual Gifts: Experiencing and Using Energy

What roles do energy and color play in your gifts?

What are the ways that energy and color speak to you?

Which color is most significant to you as your power color?

Don't Be Greedy and Forget to Ask With Gratitude

If you are trying to manifest shit in your life, no matter what it is, gratitude is the fastest way to achieve it. Visualize all that you desire, experience it as if you have already received what you want in your life: healing, a home, peace of mind.

I am so grateful for (What you desire)

I love what I have (What you desire)

Journal Shit Here

Release the Outcome and Trust in a Plan That is Better Than Your Own.

Ok my little control freaks, it's time. It's time to release control and welcome the endless possibilities into your life. So just for today, what can you let go of control so that you can allow the universe to flow in all its abundance?

Name something that you can let go of...

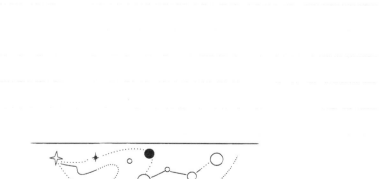

Crystals

Ignore whoever told you to buy that cotton candy poof of a crystal called rose quartz. You are going to need something stronger. Try these stones to help you on your journey.

Kyanite: Protective and gently balances the chakras.

Smokey Quartz: Grounding, physically and spiritually protective & Healing.

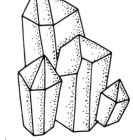

Azurite: Stone for Psychics and Mediums, enhancing your abilities.

Labradorite: Unlock your inner vision and help illuminate your path while shielding.

PS- You can color this page too!

Setting Boundaries

Ahh, my people-pleasing doormat of a spiritual human, it is time. It is time to set some strong boundaries with all those people in your life that have been taking advantage of you. It is time.

Ask yourself if you have the time, space, or energy for what is being requested of you.
Do they need your help, like their hair is on fire and they need you to pour water on it? Ooooor do they want your help, like help me bake 400 cookies tonight for the bakesale I procrastinated on and now I want your help.

If it is a need, by all means, help if you are able. There's nothing wrong with helping people. But if it's a want, ask yourself do I have the time-space and energy to do what is requested? If the answer is no, it's time to set a boundary. If the person, job, or activity drains your body, mind, and soul, it's time to say no. Try these phrases.

"Thank you for asking me, unfortunately, I'm not available for XYZ."
"I appreciate the invite, but I don't have space in my calendar." Or say "No." you don't owe any more explanation.

Journal Shit Here

Self Love

Do you remember the last thing you said to yourself when you looked in the mirror? Was it hello, you amazing sexy, badass of a spiritual human? Or was it more like hey ugly? We say shit to ourselves that we would never dream of saying to anyone else. Yet, I know that there is a beautiful and unique spiritual being that lives in that human suit you are wearing.
Look at your eyes. The color tells a story of who you are, along with your nose and every other feature of your body. We spend our lives desperately searching for our vision of perfection, what we think we need to be, look like, and act like to be successful and accepted by others. Yet, we ignore our body and subconscious, which gives us great insight into who we are and our path by looking in the mirror. I would like you to consider for a brief moment that you are perfect just the way you are. What you see as flaws is your body's way of reminding you of who you are and your mission and soul's purpose in life.

Every feature of your body says something about your eternal soul inside. For example, the first joint of your thumb should correctly measure your eye. If your eye is more significant, you tend to be more creative, smaller, and more logical. Each feature tells about you and your journey and life lessons. Those unruly curls on top of your head, or how straight your hair flows from your head, even the shape of your lips that speak your words, they all have meaning and a message about you and your soul's purpose!

What Can You Love About You Today?

A Reminder

On the first day that the first human took their first breath and looked up at the stars, they must have wondered about their existence. From the first time we saw our reflections, we were curious and excited to see the face looking back from the mirror. We smiled and laughed, loving whom we saw. We were happy little humans, enjoying our existence until someone else came along and started pointing out our imperfections.

Reality is a funny thing. We get lost in a world that transforms itself rapidly in front of our eyes, a world made up of so many points of view and filled with the opinions of other humans. We allow those opinions, self-doubts, self-loathing to overwhelm us. Desperation replaces inner peace as we search for meaning in the approval of our spouses, families, bosses, society, and we forget the most important opinion, our own.

We doubt ourselves, others, and the weather until the rain pours down on our heads. But, really doubt our doubts instead of doubting ourselves. Having faith in ourselves and our divine intuition is the ability to know the truth even though we cannot see, hear, or feel it. We have lost the ability to understand the world in a spiritual sense. Eyes blinded by opinions have lost the ability to see the beauty in the world around us and ourselves.

"Seeing is believing," they say. Skepticism is often how we meet any intangible idea. If we can't see it, we don't believe it, and often, even if we see it, we still doubt it. We often even doubt ourselves before questioning the doubts flowing within.

We are conditioned to ignore our inner power and strength. If someone else tells us it is true, it must be the truth. If the media tells us we must be a size two, have blonde hair, and perfect skin to be beautiful, that must be true as well, yes? Or maybe not?

How often do you listen to yourself? How often do you sit in stillness? Listening to the whisperings of the spirit giving you spiritual guidance, being still enough to hear the answers you seek? Do you listen to the still small voice that resides in your heart? The one that you doubt so often and constantly catch yourself saying, "I wish I would have listened to myself." You knew all along, but then you didn't know all at once.

Society teaches us to doubt ourselves, to doubt our divine intuition and capabilities. You were born of the divine, sprinkled with stardust. You have the Universe inside you. The secret messages contained in this book may be the first experience you have with reading something like this, or maybe not. Explore these pages with an open heart and mind to gain the most knowledge. Allow yourself to discover the seeds of the Universe that were planted inside you even before you were conceived. A spark of magic, the breath of God, you are a child of the Universe. You were born with a gift and a special purpose when you were born. You are not just you, but you are on a greater plane, in such magnitude and excellence, that you carry the divine inside you.

Once you learn that you can choose the outcome of your life, you will become more powerful than you could ever imagine.

What is Your Spark of Magic?

Mindless coloring, fill these lines with colors. Use the first colors you grab, no peeking. Colors have meaning. Notice what colors you chose and what they mean.

I Accept Me

Finding peace and acceptance within yourself and learning to love and appreciate all of who you are is a part of the process of understanding your purpose. You are amazing the way you are. You are perfect just the way you are. Designed with a greater and divine purpose in mind, your physical body is a reflection of your spiritual body, giving you a beautiful insight into who you are and what your soul's purpose is. Only when we realize that perfection is being exactly the way we are and fully embracing that person may we find true freedom, joy, and happiness.

Journal Shit Here

Meditation

Meditation is not sitting still and chanting Ohm. Instead, it is an innate ability to focus your energy on something other than yourself and what's going on in the world around you. It is setting aside the chaos of the world and communicating with the divine spiritual being within and spiritual world around you.

You can sit, stand, walk, sing, dance, or exercise your meditation. Clear your mind, set your intentions for your meditation, and meditate your way.

Three Deep Breaths

All you have to do is breathe. Today you can get from one breath to the next. Focus on the image on this page and take three deep breaths, filling your lungs with the breath through your nose and exhaling through your mouth. Try pausing between the inhale and exhale. It might be hard at first, but keep going. Pause and breathe for a few seconds a day, and notice how you feel.

Overcoming Anxiety Activities

1. Take a new route to the grocery store, work, school, etc.
2. Order something new on the menu the next time you eat out.
3. Do something new you have always wanted to try, take an art class, go hiking, surfing, etc.
4. Talk to a trusted friend, family member, or counselor/therapist about your anxieties.
5. Meditate.
6. Try tapping.
7. Learn more about Breathwork.
8. Try aromatherapy; essential oils such as Lavender, Lime, Patchouli, Vetiver are some of my favorites. You can grab some oils here at my.doterra.com/spiritfluent or your local health food store. Try to stick with good-quality brands like Doterra, Young Living, Rocky Mountain Oils, or Aura Cacia.
9. Try Yoga or Tai Chi.
10. Work on shifting, healing, or finding support for these common.
11. Consider leaving a stressful job or work environment.
12. Ask your doctor if your anxiety might be connected to the side effects of certain medications.
13. Heal past emotional traumas.
14. Try energy healing, EDMR therapy, or hypnosis.
15. Ditch the caffeine; it can make you jittery and increase anxiety.

Mindless coloring, fill these lines with colors. Use the first colors you grab, no peeking. Colors have meaning, notice what colors you chose and what they mean.

"Be yourself; everyone else is already taken."
— Oscar Wilde

Don't take advice from your fears. Keep faith when everything seems out of control. We all doubt ourselves or our abilities at some point. However, the difference between those who succeed in overpowering those doubts is that they don't listen to that fear monster whispering in their ear, telling them they can't do something. When we are filled with self-doubt, we can easily give up and give in to our fears. There is no true failure, just an opportunity to do things differently.

Release Your Fear

Doubt comes from fear, and fear is an unpleasant emotion caused by the belief that someone or something is dangerous or likely to cause pain or a threat. Those threats can be genuine or a bit imaginary, created in our minds after an experience scares out memories for the worse. Our subconscious minds are designed to protect us from fear, prevent us from feeling pain, and keep us out of potentially dangerous situations. However, giving in to the same fear intended to protect you also has the potential to hurt you. The same fear prevents you from listening to the still, small voice of inspiration that whispers the simple truths you need to understand in your mind.

What fear can you release today?

Journal Shit Here

Learn to listen to the still, small voice that whispers beautiful and inspired truths. This is your intuition. Before you read on, take a few minutes to clear your mind and allow yourself to connect to your intuition and the spiritual knowledge that is inside you.

Intuition is a funny thing, and it is very individual. Each person develops their way of listening to their intuition.

It is like a muscle that takes development. The more your use it, the stronger it gets.

3 Steps to Develop Intuition

The intuitive mind is a sacred gift, and the rational mind is a faithful servant. We have created a society that honors the servant and has forgotten the gift. – Albert Einstein

1. The test of objectivity.

Develop your connection with your higher power. A spiritually receptive person gets more authentic impressions than someone who lives in a physical or emotional environment not conducive to spirituality.

1. The test of Bias.

It is possible to mistake our intuition for our personal preferences and desires. Humility leads to intuition; the ego is more likely to be deceived or confused. Remove biases from your mind and let your intuition guide you...

3. Content and context are the tests.

Is this in accordance with the universal laws?
You will never be guided by intuition to act against universal laws or harm yourself or others. Your intuition will not guide you to do illegal things like rob a bank with it. This is absolutely not your intuition and is most likely a mental health concern.

Use the following prompts to write about using your intuition:

What is my intuition telling me?

Are these feelings real, or are they a reflection of my prejudices and emotions?

What actions can I take to follow my intuition?

Journal Shit Here

Trust Your Intuition

Transformation and healing go hand-in-hand, and you can't have one without the other. Everyone wants to transform their lives, but in reality, few will do the healing and the inner work necessary for lasting transformation.

You are ready for a transformation. You are prepared to learn all you can to create a beautiful life and find your success. You are ready for the real secret message, the message of truth.

The truth is, there is no magic pill, no easy button that will make your life the magical, wonderful fairytale that you always dreamed of.

As you sit there wondering what the point of this whole journal is if there is no magic pill or easy button, you may realize perceptively that you are that magical key, the easy button, the pill. But, conversely, you are also the rain that falls on your parade, the burster of your bubbles.

Ahh, yes, my friend, you are.

You are the magic, and the storm rolled all into one.

You decide what you want your life to be like.

You will decide if you take what you have learned about yourself in this book and create something magical from it, turning your proverbial lead into gold. I won't change your life, your parents won't, your partner, your kids, and winning the lottery won't. None of that will change your life.

Just as the Good Witch Glenda said in the Wizard of Oz, "You've always had the power, my dear. You just had to learn it for yourself."

So this is my challenge to you, my friend. After all, we have gone through this journal. We can call each other friends, can't we? So your challenge is to become the best person you can be, take your lemons and make the best dang lemonade you have ever tasted, because life is sweet and precious, and you were created to have joy, to be happy, and to love your life.

Become so fiercely determined and committed to this goal that nothing will deter you. Surround yourself with people who love you, support your goals, and say goodbye to those who do not.

Success is when you become self-love and accept yourself despite what others say. Success is not a number in your bank account, a prestigious job, the car you drive, or your clothes.

Success is not the size of your jeans or the number on the scale.

Success is YOU. It is within you through being yourself, just the way you are, and loving yourself just that way.

The magic is within you if you take the time to pause and understand it. Listen to yourself, your body, and your intuition.

Connect with your higher self. Listen and ask yourself, what is my path, purpose, and journey? What is your personal magic? Are you willing to release the fear that is holding it and you back from living the life you are destined for?

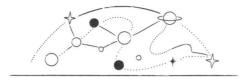

Intuition vs. Fear

Intuition and fear can sometimes overlap. If you suffer from anxiety it can be especially difficult to distinguish if your intuition or anxiety, fear, and triggers are speaking to you. These tips will help you recognize when your intuition is telling and better listen to it.

Intuition is the first spark of a beneficial or protective idea to you; a loved one, a friend, or someone else around you. It's not the overthinking or the self-doubt that follows. So remember, doubt your doubts before you doubt your intuition.

Your intuition will never lead you to do something harmful to yourself or others. There is a fine line between spiritual and mental health. And if the spiritual starts to affect your mental health or daily life, it's time to get support.

There's nothing like intuition. It's a whisper on your heart, a whisper of a voice in your ear, a tingle down your spine, a feather in your path. It looks and feels different for everyone, but once you learn your intuition and follow it, you'll be amazed at the results.

Intuitive Day

Listen to all the good things your intuition guides you towards today. Follow those sparks of intuition. Journal about it here.

Shit I'm Grateful For

SHIT THAT MAKES ME HAPPY

1. ....
2. ....
3. ....

SHIT THAT MAKES ME GRATEFUL

1. ....
2. ....
3. ....

EVEN THOUGH LIFE FEELS LIKE A SHIT SHOW, WHAT IS GOOD ABOUT TODAY

Mindless coloring, fill these lines with colors. Use the first colors you grab, no peeking. Colors have meaning. Notice what colors you chose and what they mean.

Trauma & Spirituality

There is a connection to those with spiritual gifts and trauma. It seems that these unpleasant life experiences are connected in a way to our spiritual gifts. Some of the greatest challenges and gifts are given to the strongest of souls. Releasing your trauma can help you heal. Go within and see/feel your trauma and then draw or journal about it here.

Journal Prompts

Healing Trauma journal prompts:

Are there ways in which you can use your experience to help others?

_____
_____
_____

Name 10 ways you can start taking better care of yourself.

_____
_____
_____

Something I am judging/blaming/shaming myself over is:

_____
_____
_____
_____
_____
_____

Watch or listen to the Ocean of Healing Meditation on the Spirit Fluent Youtube channel and journal about your experience.

Rest, Retreat, & Restore

As we are on our spiritual awakening journey, we rush to finish the process. "That's enough lessons," we say to the universe. Healing and spiritual progression come in cycles. We must learn and process. There needs to be a rest, retreat, and restoring period for our body, mind, and soul to pause and allow healing to occur.

What can I do to rest today?

What can I do to retreat and go within today?

What can I do to restore my body, mind, or soul today?

Small Simple Things

It is often the seemingly small things combined over a long period of time that bring about big things. Small and simple shifts in our lives will lift us to great things. Remember that your soul's purpose can be achieved through small, simple, and consistent actions rather than spectacular and momentous events. What are some small, simple things you can shift in your life today?

I give myself permission to create what I need to create and align with my purpose.
I give myself permission to feel what I need to feel, the good, bad, the ugly.
I give myself permission to breathe in this day and fully experience it.
I give myself permission to feel powerful.
I give myself permission to trust who I am.
I give myself permission to feel my power, lifting me like a warm wind into new experiences of self and identity.
I give myself permission to fly higher than I've ever flown before.
I give myself permission to try harder than I've ever tried before.
I give myself permission to fail.
I give myself permission to succeed.
It's okay to be right where I am, wherever I might be, between those mythic, drifting poles.
I give myself permission to be unsure about what I'm doing here.
I give myself permission to trust in the unknowable value of my unique purpose.
I give myself permission to be myself.
I give myself permission to be present in my reality right now.
This room. This body. This being.
I give myself permission to call it good.
I give myself permission to call myself worthy.
My divine worth is undeniable.
I give myself permission to still know who I am, even when I'm lost and unsure.
I don't look outside, hoping someone else will save me.
Instead, I give myself permission to save myself and know who I am.

What if you allowed yourself to dream, to explore the infinite possibilities, to become something else other than what you are right now?

Surrender

Surrending to a destiny greater than we ever thought imaginable takes a sprinkle of bravery and a whole lot of trust. What can you surrender to today?

"If you wish to understand the Universe, think of energy, frequency, and vibration."
—Nikola Tesla

Energy permeates every part of our world. Everything is made up of vibrating blobs of energy at a microscopic level. So everything vibrates, helping you fill the Universe with the amazingness that is you.

Color Me

Chakras

The body has hundreds of chakras. Most people will teach about the primary seven chakras, and all you need to know to start is Thanos. However, understand that every organ has multiple chakras, and every joint has a chakra. Your heart has two chakras your liver has three. Head to my Youtube channel, where I have free classes on chakras and how to heal them. All you need to know about chakras today is that they are energetic exchange systems similar to breathing. Drawing in clean energy to your spiritual body and expelling old energy. Sometimes they get blocked or stop functioning due to trauma or emotional experiences.

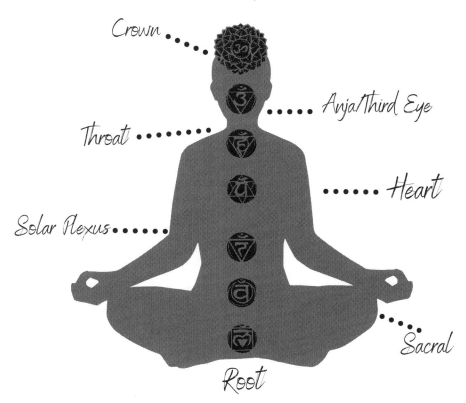

Chakra Journaling Questions

Crown: How can I more completely connect to Creator?
Anja: Can I trust my inner knowing?
Throat: How can I use healing words to speak my truth in a valuable way?
Heart: Can I release the protection I have surrounding my heart and allow love to flow again?
Solar Plexus: Can I trust my gut instincts enough to let go of worry or fear?
Sacral: What shame, humiliation, or anger can I release?
Root: What are some of my deepest/most beautiful memories?

For those with the third eye open to using intuition, it is by far superior to any other form of intuition or spiritual gift. It is your inner bullshit detector, and you know the truths from fiction. You will gain a deeper understanding of life and your purpose if you use intuition and intellect in a coordinated, objective, and effective manner. Developing inner knowing is an essential part of our journey.

Your inner wisdom can help you restore harmony in your third eye chakra by opening yourself to new ideas and understanding. Knowledge may come from others or may come from within yourself.

The element of light significantly influences the third eye's chakra. Sunlight is one source, but the stars and the moon also emit light to balance your chakras. A walk on a sunny day or in the evening of a full moon can assist in restoring the third eye chakra balance.

Balance your third eye chakra by:

Physical Activity and movement
Prayer and Meditation

Affirmations:

I am in touch with my inner guidance
I am intuitive
I trust my intuition

Aromatherapy:

Clary Sage, Pine, Frankincense, Ylang Ylang, Lavender, Patchouli, Cedar

Shit I'm Grateful For

SHIT THAT MAKES ME HAPPY

1. ....
2. ....
3. ....

SHIT THAT MAKES ME GRATEFUL

1. ....
2. ....
3. ....

EVEN THOUGH LIFE FEELS LIKE A SHIT SHOW, WHAT IS GOOD ABOUT TODAY

Journal Shit Here

The 12 Universal Laws

No matter what your belief system is, there are Universal Laws that apply to every one of us. Those Universal laws dictate how life flows around us. Understanding these concepts will help you know why you have a birthmark, how they came to be, how they affect us, and what they mean for your journey here on Earth.

There are 12 Universal Laws that are constant, unchanged, and everlasting. The most famous of those laws is the Law of Attraction. I bet you didn't know there are more laws than the law of attraction, did you? The 12 Universal Laws exist to create balance, harmony, and flow in our existence, the Earth, and Everything around us. They are unchanging and unbreakable. If you learn to live your life in harmony with these laws, you will notice that your life may start to flow with more ease. A basic review of these laws can help you to have a deeper understanding of why the knowledge behind your birthmarks is so essential to living a successful life and fulfilling your soul purpose.

1. The Law of Oneness

"We are all one," the bottle of my Dr. Bronner's soap proudly exclaims. Dr. Bronner felt that if people stopped focusing on our differences and instead thought about how we are the same, we would all be better off on this "Spaceship Earth," as he called it. First Nations People believe that "all things are connected." Scientists refer to it as the "unified field." You can go deep into the quantum physics rabbit hole to learn more. I am not an expert in this field, so we are just going to touch on the importance of understanding this by letting Albert Einstein explain the concept:

"A human being is a part of the whole, called by us, 'Universe,' a part limited in time and space. He experiences himself, thoughts, and feelings as something separated from the rest... a kind of optical delusion of his consciousness. This delusion is a kind of prison for us, restricting us to our desires and affection for a few persons nearest to us. Our task must be to free ourselves from this prison by widening our circle of compassion to embrace all living creatures and the whole of nature in its beauty. Of course, nobody can achieve this completely, but the striving for such achievement is in itself a part of the liberation and a foundation for inner security."

The Law of Oneness states Everything is connected in this world... every person, object, situation. We are all one, connected in a great web of weirdness. So yeah, it took me a bit to digest this too.

"Whatever affects one directly affects all indirectly. I can never be what I ought to be until you are what you ought to be. This is the interrelated structure of reality." - Martin Luther King, Jr.

Journal Shit Here

Journal Shit Here

2. The Law of Energy or Vibration

"The energy of the mind is the essence of life." – Aristotle
We have already touched a bit on energy. In a nutshell, We can explain the Law of Energy/Vibration as Everything vibrates at its frequency.

$E=mc^2$. Everyone has heard this famous theorem, but few understand what it means. Einstein's formula illustrates that matter (i.e., tangible things like humans, trees, rocks, etc.) and energy are the same things. The energy and matter are converted to life force energy, like Qi and prana. Think about how plants turn light into energy during photosynthesis. New Age thinking and quantum physics converge in the Law of Vibration.

Energy and vibrations are constantly being sent out into the Universe. You, plants, trees, and animals all send out our energy like radio signals from one car to another. The Law of Energy says that energy is constantly in motion, flowing on many frequency levels. Everything is made of energy, even you.

Try going outside. Look at the trees or grass around you. Then look up at the sky. You may see little tiny balls of light floating around you like sparkly dust. This is energy, Qi, or prana.

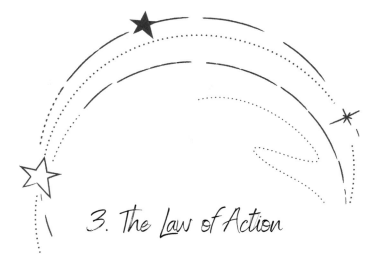

3. The Law of Action

"Willing is not enough. We must do." – Johann Von Goethe.
As you will start to learn about your birthmarks in the following chapters, you will also begin to learn about shifting your life using the secret messages your birthmark carries. Taking action is vital to manifest your new and fantastic reality to use that information. Active participation includes activities that support our thoughts, dreams, emotions, and words. The Law of Action states that you must do the things and perform the actions necessary to achieve what you are setting out to do.

As my distant cousin twice removed (or something like that), Isaac Newton devised in his Third Law: there is an equal and opposite reaction for every action. Your actions create responses throughout the Universe. Like tossing a rock into a pond, the ripples can go on and on. The bigger the stone you throw (i.e., the action), the bigger the splash you will make (i.e., the results). Keep this in mind.

Journal Shit Here

Journal Shit Here

4. The Law of Correspondence

No, this law is not about writing a letter to your grandmother. Instead, let's take a field trip. Grab this book and head to the bathroom. Okay, now look in the mirror. What you see reflected on the outside is what is on the inside. This is the most important of all the Laws that connect with your body features.

"As above, so below." Our dimensional eternal being is being actively reflected through the features of our body... yes, even though your body features. Talk about wearing your heart on your sleeve! Every feature says something about who you are as a spiritual being.

This law is also reflected in our lives as a whole... how we live, our emotions, where we find ourselves living, working, etc. What we create in our subconscious mind creates the reality we live within. This was a big pill for me to swallow. The first time I heard this, I got outraged and said to myself, "What do you mean I create my reality? All this chaos around me, I didn't want this!"

Yet, through your subconscious emotions, you did create it. Remember, your decisions determine your destiny.

We cannot control what happens to us, but we can control how we react. Therefore, our reactions (emotional outbursts from our subconscious mind) are reflected in what happens next.

Like the Choose Your Adventure books I read as a kid, we are literally choosing our own adventure when it comes to our lives.

5. The Law of Cause and Effect

Actions, or inactions, are put into motion by every thought, word, or deed. The Law of Cause and Effect is perpetually in motion like a swinging pendulum seeking balance. Again to reference Newton, "For every action, there is an equal and opposite reaction."

Your actions create reactions throughout the Universe, like when you are swimming, the amount of force used while you swim the breaststroke. Recitation and movement force more research.

There is a cause for every effect and an effect for every cause. This law states there are no coincidences. That Everything happens in life for a reason, even if we can not always figure out why or how. When something is happening in my life, I pause and ask myself, "What is the purpose of this experience?"

I have found that the faster I learn, the faster I can move away from some of life's more unpleasant teaching moments.

This is the Law of Cause and Effect.

Journal Shit Here

Journal Shit Here

6. The Law of Compensation

I am sure you have noticed by now that these laws are closely connected. As The Law of Cause and Effect, The Law of Compensation describes what we put out, we get back. If we give, we receive. Good or bad, those things will eventually come back to us. It may not happen instantaneously, but I have found the Universe has a way of working things out. There is a right time to give and a suitable time to receive, and they don't always match up. This law takes a lot of patience and often a lot of time to see the results. But, have no fear, my friend. It will always match up. You will always be rewarded for your efforts or lack thereof. You may have heard of people talking about Karma or "what you reap, you sow." From so many life experiences, I have learned that this is completely and utterly true.

"For every thing you have missed, you have gained something else; and for every thing you gain, you lose something. If riches increase, they are increased that use them. If the gatherer gathers too much, nature takes out of the man what she puts into his chest; swells the estate, but kills the owner. Nature hates monopolies and exceptions." – Ralph Waldo Emerson.

7. The Law of Attraction

"Once you make a decision, the Universe conspires to make it happen." --Ralph Waldo Emerson

You have the power. You have to control your reality with the help of the Universe.

Look around the room you are in right now. Everything in front of you has been attracted to your reality through the energy you radiate. The core of your beliefs, your thoughts, people, and actions radiate out and draw that reality to you.

Ralph Trine wrote in In Tune With The Infinite (1897):
The law of attraction works universally on every plane of action, and we attract whatever we desire or expect. If we choose one thing and expect another, we become like houses divided against themselves, quickly brought to desolation. Determine resolutely to expect only what you desire. Then you will attract only what you wish for

"Ask, and ye shall receive." The Law of Attraction is the most often taught of the 12 Laws, but if you ignore the other 11 laws, you will have a pretty tough time attracting what you ask for. So many people flock to the Law of Attraction because it sounds so easy... manifest your desires! But then, when it fails, it leaves a trail of disbelievers in its path. My friends, you can not pick and choose which laws of the Universe you follow, for if you do, you will lack success.

Journal Shit Here

Journal Shit Here

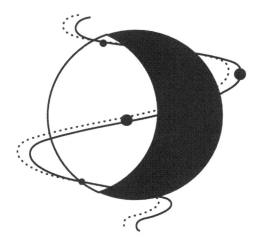

8. The Law of Perpetual Transmutation of Energy

This is one of my favorite laws because after all those heavy laws telling us we had direct influence over our lives, it's nice to know we can change what we don't like. Thank goodness, right? This is my personal favorite of all the laws. It tells me I have the power within me to change anything in my world. Yes, I like that quite a lot.

Just as you can create your life, you also can change it. Give the Universe a big "no, thank you" to the stuff you don't like and order something new on that Universal menu. Our energy and the energy around us are in constant motion (thanks for the gem, Einstein!), so we can choose how that energy flows or away from us. Don't like the direction your life is going? Just change it up by doing something different or opposite to what you usually do.

9. The Law of Relativity

Think of life as a big school where we are constantly taught and tested. This cycle repeats itself. You may have noticed the same things in your life happening over and over. This is a massive opportunity for growth in our lives. It impacts how we see and think about the things around us. If you can change your perspective, you can change your life! Is the glass half empty or half full? You decide. Einstein dropped so many gems, including the First Law, that there is no "absolute" frame of reference. Everything that happens to us could be happening for us.

According to this law, we tend to compare things in our world, but in actuality, everything is neutral. Thus, our actions and reactions to our experiences give them energy.

How can bad things be happening for us?
To inspire growth and learning or make our lives miserable is all from your perspective.

We have a short time here on Earth and only a short amount of time to grow as spiritual beings. So take the time to learn all you can, even from the bad. Find love and support as you grow into the beautiful spiritual being you were destined to be. Just as a student needs a teacher, look for a guide who can support you as you experience the ups and downs of life.

It's all relative, baby.

Journal Shit Here

Journal Shit Here

"To Everything (turn, turn, turn)

There is a season (turn, turn, turn)
And a time to every purpose, under heaven
A time to be born, a time to die
A time to plant, a time to reap
A time to kill, a time to heal
A time to laugh, a time to weep
To Everything (turn, turn, turn)
There is a season (turn, turn, turn)
And a time to every purpose, under heaven
A time to build up, a time to break down
A time to dance, a time to mourn
A time to cast away stones, a time to gather stones together
To Everything (turn, turn, turn)
There is a season (turn, turn, turn)
And a time to every purpose, under heaven
A time of love, a time of hate
A time of war, a time of peace
A time you may embrace, a time to refrain from embracing
To Everything (turn, turn, turn)
There is a season (turn, turn, turn)
And a time to every purpose under the heaven
A time to gain, a time to lose
A time to rend, a time to sew
A time for love, a time for hate
A time for peace, I swear it's not too late."

– Peter Seeger., Songwriter.

11. The Law of Rhythm

Like a pendulum swinging back and forth, the Universe desires balance. If that balance is disrupted, the pendulum will swing wildly, in the opposite direction, to find balance again. Within this Law is the message that begs us to keep nature and the Universe in harmony, reminding us not to do things that create imbalances. Creating imbalance will have its consequences.

Emerson spoke about this in his 1841 writing of Compensation, "The absolute balance of Giving and Take, the doctrine that everything has its price —and if that price is not paid, not that thing but something else is obtained, and that it is impossible to get anything without its price — is not less sublime in the columns of a ledger than in the budgets of states, in the laws of light and darkness, in all the action and reaction of nature."
As we observe sunrises and sunsets, we can see this.
As the tide goes in and out, so does the ebb and flow.

Life cycles are the subject of this Law. There is a natural rhythm to everything. When you allow yourself to flow with this universal rhythm, you will balance your life.

Journal Shit Here

Journal Shit Here

12. The Law of Gender

Yin and Yang is the most commonly understood symbol of the Law of Gender. Everything has masculine and feminine energy. The Law of Gender manifests in our world regardless of gender identification. There are ways you can possess and express both feminine and masculine energy. This Law decrees that Everything in nature is both male and female. Both are required for life to exist. Everything contains this principle in them.

For the Law of Gender to work for you, you need to recognize what energy, masculine or feminine, you possess the most. You will find that it is much easier to channel the opposite energy when you identify what energy you mainly carry yourself with.

Grab a piece of paper and stand in front of a mirror. First, hold the form in front of the left side of your face and observe the right side of your face. Then move the paper to cover the right side and observe your left. You may have observed that your left side looks slightly feminine and the right a bit more masculine. Neat, right?

I mention these universal laws to help you better understand the Universe around you and how the intention of divinity works. There is often an unbalanced focus on the Law of Attraction, and people do not know that they need to have harmony and balance with all 12 rules, not just one, for their lives to flow with more ease.

If you have a bit of an understanding of the energy and the Universe around you, it may help you gain a greater understanding of why your birthmarks are more than the flaws you have always perceived them to be. If you could believe for a brief moment in time that there is a greater force working around you and for you, then maybe, just maybe, you can find that you are flawless and powerful just the way the Universe created you.

Journal Shit Here

Journal Shit Here

Journal Shit Here

Journal Shit Here

Journal Shit Here

Journal Shit Here

Journal Shit Here

Journal Shit Here

Journal Shit Here

Journal Shit Here

Journal Shit Here

Journal Shit Here

Journal Shit Here

Journal Shit Here

Journal Shit Here

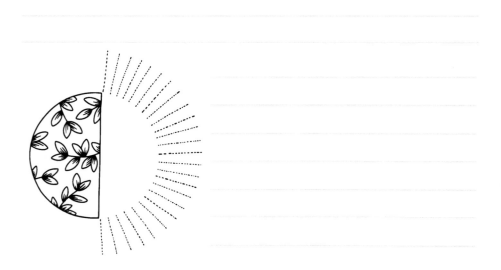

Journal Shit Here

Journal Shit Here

Journal Shit Here

Journal Shit Here

Journal Shit Here

Journal Shit Here

Journal Shit Here

Journal Shit Here

Congratulations!

Well done my Spiritual Human! You have reached the end of this Journal. If you are ready to continue your journey with me as your guide, join me on my website for more classes to help you heal and develop your spiritual gifts.

www.SpiritFluent.com

Follow me on all social media at @SpiritFluent

Love,
Stacee

About Me

I am a spiritual human on a journey just like anyone else. In 2016, I had a profound spiritual awakening that changed the course of my life forever. For as long as I can remember, I've had my spiritual gifts. However, these reawakened long-buried spiritual gifts within me that had been suppressed for years. I went from running my own manufacturing business to an ever-evolving spiritual human just like you. The path of my life has been filled with ups and downs. One thing I know is that if I can make one person's life better by knowing me, then I have succeeded. I invite you to take this journey with me.